Date: 11/8/21

J BIO OBAMA
Shaffer, Jody Jensen,
Barack Obama : first African
American president /

BARACK OBAMA

FIRST AFRICAN AMERICAN PRESIDENT

"Change will not come
if we wait for some other person
or if we wait for some other time.
We are the ones we've been waiting for.
We are the change that we seek. "
— Barack Obama —

BY JODY JENSEN SHAFFER

Published by The Child's World®
1980 Lookout Drive, Mankato, MN 56003-1705
800-599-READ • www.childsworld.com

PHOTOS

Cover and page 4: AP Photo/Isaac Brekken
Interior:
AP Photo/Morry Gash: 5; AP Photo/Nam Y. Huh: 15; AP Photo/Pablo Martinez
Monsivais: 25; AP Photo/Ron Edmonds: 20; AP Photo/Susan Walsh: 24; Ashlee
Rezin/Chicago Sun-Times via AP: 26; Courtesy Barack Obama Presidential Library:
8; GRANGER: 13; Harry E. Walker/TNS/Newscom: 19; Joe Raedle/Getty Images
News via Getty Images: 17; Joe Wrinn/Harvard University/Corbis via Getty Images:
11; John Gress/Reuters/Newscom: 18, 31; Obama Press Office/UPI/Newscom: 6, 7,
9, 10, 28 (both); Obama-Robinson Family Archive: 12; Official White House Photo
by Annie Leibovitz/Courtesy Barack Obama Presidential Library: 21; Pete Souza/
KRT/Newscom: 14; US National Archives and Records Administration: 23, 27

LIBRARY OF CONGRESS CATALOGING-IN-PUBLICATION DATA
ISBN 9781503853775 (Reinforced Library Binding)
ISBN 9781503853997 (Portable Document Format)
ISBN 9781503854116 (Online Multi-user eBook)
LCCN: 2020943592

Printed in the United States of America

Cover and page 4 caption:
President Barack Obama
speaking at a high school
in Las Vegas in 2013.

CONTENTS

Chapter One

FROM HAWAII TO INDONESIA

On November 4, 2008, Barack Obama made history. He was elected the 44th president of the United States. He was the first African American to hold the office. It was a dream he'd had since third grade. He knew being president wouldn't be easy. America was in a huge financial crisis. It was fighting two wars overseas. But Obama, a Democrat, thought he could help. He believed America was ready for change.

Obama stood on stage in Chicago's Grant Park and claimed victory. "If there is anyone out there who still doubts that America is a place where all things are possible; who still wonders if the dream of our founders is alive in our time; who still questions the power of our **democracy**, tonight is your answer." "It's been a long time coming, but tonight, because of what we did on this day, in this election, at this defining moment, change has come to America."

Barack Obama waves at his election-night party on November 4, 2008.

Barack Hussein Obama was born on August 4, 1961 in Honolulu, Hawaii. His father, also named Barack Obama, was a Black man from Kenya. Kenya is a country in Africa. Barack's father went to college at the University of Hawaii. He was its first African student. Barack's mother, Ann Dunham, was a white woman who was born in Fort Leavenworth, Kansas. She moved with her parents to Hawaii in 1959. Ann also attended the University of Hawaii. Barack's parents met in Russian class. They were married in 1960. They divorced when Barack was two.

Barack means "blessed" in the Swahili language.

Barack and his mom lived with her parents, Stanley and Madelyn Dunham. Barack called them "Gramps" and "Toot." When Barack was six, his mother married again. Lolo Soetoro was a college student from Indonesia. He and Barack got along well. In 1967 the family moved to Jakarta, Indonesia. That was Lolo's hometown.

When Barack first arrived in Jakarta, Lolo surprised him with a gift. It was an ape named Tata! It had come from New Guinea. Lolo's back yard was filled with animals. He had chickens and ducks, a big yellow dog, birds, and two baby crocodiles.

Young Barack in Honolulu, Hawaii.

Neither Barack nor his mom knew the language spoken in Jakarta. But it only took Barack six months to learn it. He went to both a government-run school and a private school. He also took classes that came by mail. Barack's mom wanted Barack to keep his education up to American grade levels. Every morning at 4AM, she taught Barack English for three hours. Then he went to his Indonesian school. In a class assignment in third grade, he wrote that he wanted to be president when he grew up.

Barack had lots of fun in Jakarta. His friends were children of servants, farmers, and government workers. Together they caught crickets, battled with **swift kites**, and took odd jobs. His friends helped him try snake meat and roasted grasshoppers. His stepfather taught him to box to protect himself.

It was a life of adventure for Barack. But he knew life was hard for other people, like the poor and sick who begged at their door. It bothered him that there was such a big gap between people who had money and those who didn't.

Throughout his childhood and into college, Barack was known as Barry. On the first day of fifth grade, his teacher asked if he wanted to be called Barry or Barack. The kids laughed at his Kenyan name. When he started high school, he told his teachers, "Just call me Barry." But when he got to New York to attend Columbia University, he asked people to call him Barack. "It was not some assertion of my African roots ... not a racial assertion. It was much more...that I was coming of age...that I was comfortable with the fact that I was different and that I didn't need to try to fit in in a certain way," he later wrote.

Obama and his family in Indonesia.

After a few years in Jakarta, Barack's mom became concerned for her son's safety and education. She and Lolo split up. In 1971 when Barack was ten, she sent him back to Hawaii to live with his grandparents. Barack's half-sister, Maya, was born in 1970. She stayed in Indonesia with their mom. She was studying to be an **anthropologist**. They would join Barack later that year.

In Hawaii, Barack interviewed for and was accepted into Punahou School. He would be in fifth grade. Barack was one of very few Black kids in school. He felt the sting of **racism** from time to time.

When Barack was ten, his father visited from Kenya. Barack hadn't seen his father since he was two. Barack's father

Barack Obama Sr. visited Hawaii when Barack was 10 years old.

spoke to Barack's class. The students were fascinated with his stories. Barack's dad stayed for a month. He gave Barack his first basketball. It was the last time Barack saw his father. He died in a car accident in Kenya eleven years later. Barack's mother went back to Indonesia to continue studying. Barack and Maya stayed in Hawaii. Barack played basketball after school on a playground near their apartment.

Barack started high school at Punahou in 1975. He was one of just five or six Black kids in his high school. Barack was a good student, but not great. He worked part-time at an ice cream shop. He played tennis and varsity basketball, though he was often benched. As Barack continued through high school, he began to wonder where he fit in racially. He started to read Black authors such as James Baldwin, Ralph Ellison, and Langston Hughes.

Obama loves sports. As a child he surfed, swam, and boxed. He played basketball throughout his youth and adulthood.

In 1976, Barack's mom and sister went back to Indonesia. Barack stayed with his grandparents. It was hard. His relationship with his grandfather was sometimes strained. There were not many Black males to serve as role models in Hawaii. He later wrote, "I was trying to raise myself to be a Black man in America and…no one around me seemed to know exactly what that meant." In 1979 Barack graduated from Punahou. He won a **scholarship** to attend Occidental College in Los Angeles.

Barack playing basketball at Punahou School in Honolulu in 1979.

Chapter Two

FROM LOS ANGELES TO CHICAGO

Barack met several other Black students at Occidental. He participated in student protests. He also began taking leadership positions. He was asked to speak at a rally on campus. Even though his part of the program was only a few minutes, he was a big success. People listened to his opinions. It made him "hungry for words." He was beginning to see his unique position as an American. He was part of both Black and white American families. He saw their doubts, fear, and dreams. Later that year, he learned that Occidental had a transfer program with Columbia University in New York City. Barack applied and was accepted. He began in the fall of 1981.

In New York, he started getting more serious about life. He ran three miles a day. He fasted on Sundays. He read books and took long walks. He studied, and he kept a journal of "daily reflections and very bad poetry," he said later.

Barack in New York in the early 1980s.

He had a summer job clearing a construction site. Barack graduated with a Political Science degree in 1983. He took a job as a community organizer in Harlem. Later he was a research assistant and editor. He didn't enjoy the work.

Then in 1985 he was offered a job in Chicago, Illinois. He would be a community organizer. He would try to improve living conditions for inner-city residents. Obama interviewed community members about their problems. He was paid ten thousand dollars for the first year. He got two-thousand-dollars to buy a car. He enjoyed the work but discovered it was hard to get things done without a law degree. He didn't feel "there would be large-scale change brought about by organizing."

Obama at Harvard Law School.

In the fall of 1988, at age 27, Obama decided to get a law degree. He was accepted into Harvard Law School in Cambridge, Massachusetts. Before he began, he traveled to Kenya to meet his extended family. He stayed for several weeks.

Obama was much older than his classmates at Harvard. He was an excellent student. He was a research assistant for one of his professors his first semester. When he spoke in class, everyone paid attention. He was respected by his peers and teachers.

In the summer after his first year at Harvard, Obama worked as an intern in a Chicago law office. Michelle Robinson was his boss. She was three years younger. She had also attended Harvard. Obama wanted to date Michelle, but she wasn't sure. After a company picnic, he offered to buy her ice cream. She agreed. They dated long-distance when he returned to Harvard.

In 1990, Obama became the first African American elected president of *Harvard Law Review*. He got a contract with a publisher to write a book about race. *Dreams from My Father: A Story of Race and Inheritance* was published in 1995. He graduated **magna cum laude** with his law degree in 1991. He and Michelle married on October 3, 1992 at Trinity United Church of Christ in Chicago.

The Obamas as a young couple.

Obama organized Chicago voters in Project Vote! during the 1992 elections.

Many past presidents of *Harvard Law Review* clerked with the Supreme Court or practiced law at a big firm. Obama didn't want that. He wanted to "try to do things to improve society" instead. He wanted to "pursue [his] dreams and give something back." In 1992, Obama helped register 150,000 voters in Illinois. Then he worked on civil rights cases, writing briefs and contracts. He also taught Constitutional law at the University of Chicago Law School and gave speeches around Chicago.

Chapter Three

POLITICS AND FAMILY

Obama felt he could help America even more as a public official. In 1995 he ran for the state senate in Illinois. He won! He served Chicago's 13th district, the South Side. He was reelected in 1998 and 2002, spending a total of 8 years in the Illinois **legislature**. During that time, he sponsored more than 700 bills. Almost two-thirds were signed into law. His bills helped children, the elderly, labor unions, and the poor.

Then on July 4, 1998, the Obamas' first daughter, Malia Ann, was born. Obama continued to work in the Illinois senate. But he was getting restless. He wanted to make bigger changes for people, not just in Illinois but throughout America. In 2000, he ran for a United States congressional seat. He lost badly.

Senator Obama heads up the Capitol steps to vote on a bill.

A second baby, Natasha (called "Sasha"), was born in June 2001. The Obamas were busy with their careers and parenthood. The couple worked together to care for their girls. Michelle's mother, Marian Robinson, helped, too.

In September 2001, Obama decided to run for another political office. This time, he would run for the United States Senate. He told Michelle it would be his "one last shot to test out my ideas before I settled into a calmer, more stable, better paying existence." She agreed, but she joked that she didn't promise to vote for him.

Obama was a good speaker. In 2002, he gave a speech opposing the American invasion of Iraq. "I don't oppose all wars… What I am opposed to is a dumb war. What I am opposed to is a rash war." People found his speech moving. Many who hadn't heard of him noticed his ability to move listeners.

> Obama loves to play Scrabble and poker. He also reads and writes extensively. He collects Spider-Man and Conan the Barbarian comics.

The Obama family (Malia in green and Sasha in blue) in 2004.

Another speech made Obama even more well-known. In 2004, he gave a speech at the Democratic National Convention. In it, he said, "There's not a **liberal** America and a **conservative** America…There's a United States of America. There's not a Black America and white America and Latino America and Asian America. There's a United States of America." He spoke about his background and heritage. He spoke about coming together as a country. He spoke of change and hope. He inspired many people.

In November 2004, Obama was elected to the U.S. Senate with 70% of the vote. He became only the fifth African American to serve in the U.S. Senate. He was sworn into office on January 3, 2005 as a member of the 109th Congress. He rented an apartment in Washington, DC. He hated to be away from Michelle and the girls and called them frequently. He stayed in DC three nights a week, then joined them in Chicago on the weekends.

As a senator, Obama worked with Republicans and Democrats. He worked to destroy weapons of mass destruction, which some countries use against enemies to destroy entire cities or areas. Obama focused on issues such as **lobbying** and ethics reform. He pushed for alternative energy development.

In 2006, he published *The Audacity of Hope: Thoughts on Reclaiming the American Dream.* It became a national bestseller. People of all races, ages, and economic backgrounds could identify with it. In the book, Obama talks about his faith, politics, the Constitution, and race. Then, in February of 2007, he announced he would run for president of the United States.

Chapter Four

BECOMING PRESIDENT

America was having a hard time in 2008. It was going through
the worst **recession** since the **Great Depression**. It was fighting
wars in Iraq and Afghanistan. Obama wanted to help. He ran
his campaign differently than most politicians. He didn't accept
money from the government. Instead, he raised millions of dollars
on the Internet from millions of ordinary Americans." He chose
Joe Biden as his running mate. They would face Republicans
John McCain and Sarah Palin in the general election.

Obama launched his
campaign tour alongside Joe
Biden on August 23, 2008.

Obama campaigned on reforming America's financial industry. He talked about creating different kinds of energy. He wanted to reinvent education and health care. And he wanted to bring down the national debt. It was an ambitious agenda. But many people supported him. He had a natural **charisma** and a message of hope and change that inspired large crowds. His campaign team worked to bring new, young voters to the polls. Then, on November 4, 2008, Obama made history! He was elected president of the United States. He was the first African American to ever hold the office.

Obama waves as he takes the stage at a campaign rally in 2008.

Obama places his hand on the Lincoln Bible as he takes the oath of office.

The Obamas rented a house until they could move into the White House in January. Michelle's mother planned to move to the White House, too. When school started for Malia and Sasha in January 2009, they attended Sidwell Friends School. Sasha was in second grade. Malia was in fifth.

Obama was just 47-years old when he was sworn in as 44th president of the United States on January 20, 2009. In his inauguration speech he said, "Today I say to you that the challenges we face are real. They are serious and they are many. They will not be met easily or in a short span of time. But know this, America: They will be met."

President Obama watches as Malia walks Bo in April of 2009.

One of his first challenges was to keep a promise to Malia and Sasha. Obama said they could have a dog if he won the election. Shortly after they moved into the White House, Bo joined them. He was a Portuguese water dog. He was a gift from Senator Ted Kennedy. In 2013, Sunny, a second Portuguese water dog, joined the family.

Obama loved his girls and wanted to be a good father. He played outside with them during snowy winters. He swung with them on their swing set in the summer. He sometimes coached Sasha's basketball team. He cheered as Malia played soccer. He shot water guns with them on vacation.

People asked if being president made it hard to spend time with his family. Obama said it made life easier! He and Michelle blocked off time for the family. Dinnertime at 6:30PM was one of those times. "My staff knows that it pretty much takes a national emergency to keep me away from that dinner table," Obama wrote.

Obama loves kids. When he was in the White House, he encouraged staff to bring their kids in to visit him. He marveled at Halloween costumes and held babies. One famous picture shows a little Black boy feeling Obama's hair to see if it was like his. In 2010, Obama wrote a children's book for Malia and Sasha called *Of Thee I Sing: A Letter to My Daughters*.

The Obamas sit for a photo in the Green Room of the White House in 2009.

As president, Obama expanded health insurance for children. He worked to ensure women got equal pay for equal work. He passed a bill to help the economy. He helped the struggling auto industry. He put new regulations on banks. He cut taxes on working families. He provided money for science. He created the Patient Protection and Affordable Care Act (often called "Obamacare"). It gave health insurance to millions of Americans. He proposed gun control. He reached out to foreign governments. In October 2009, Obama was awarded the Nobel Peace Prize for "his extraordinary efforts to strengthen international diplomacy and cooperation between peoples."

Empathy has always guided Obama's decisions—before, during, and after his presidency. His mom taught him empathy by asking, "How would that make you feel?" He continues to live by the Golden Rule—do unto others as you would have them do unto you.

But he had more to do! In 2012, Obama ran for president again. This time he faced Republicans Mitt Romney and Paul Ryan. Obama won again! In his victory speech Obama said, "Democracy in a nation of 300 million can be noisy and messy and complicated...[but] we are not as divided as our politics suggest. We're not as cynical as the pundits believe. We are greater than the sum of our individual ambitions."

President Obama continued to tackle tough issues. He condemned Syria for using chemical weapons on its citizens. He made sure inspectors got to see inside Iran's nuclear plants. Obama was the first sitting U.S. president to speak to the British Parliament. He also visited Hiroshima, Japan, where the world's first nuclear strike took place. And he re-established relations with Cuba and other foreign countries.

President Obama, Vice President Joe Biden, and other White House staffers celebrate the passage of the Affordable Care Act in 2010.

Obama was given the code name "Renegade" by his Secret Service duty. Maybe because he liked to drop in, unexpected, to talk with citizens as he traveled.

Obama's presidency was coming to a close. He started making plans for after he left the White House. In March 2016 he announced that his family would remain in Washington, DC until Sasha finished high school in 2019. Malia had decided to attend Harvard in 2017, after taking a gap year after high school. The Obamas rented and later bought a house in Washington.

President Obama signing several acts in 2016.

Chapter Five

AFTER THE WHITE HOUSE

Obama served as U.S. president for eight years, the limit allowed by the Constitution. In January 2017, he gave his farewell address in Chicago. "I'm asking you to believe. Not in my ability to bring about change—but in yours." In a personal goodbye to his White House team he wrote, "America is not the project of any one person. The single most powerful word in our democracy is the word 'We.' 'We the People.' 'We shall overcome.'" Later that day, as his helicopter flew away from the White House for the last time, he looked down and said, "We used to live there."

President Obama delivering his farewell address in Chicago on January 10, 2017.

Obama has been busy with family and projects. In 2017, he unveiled plans for his future presidential center in Chicago. It will include a library, museum, athletic facility, and forum for public meetings."

In August of that year, he helped move Malia into her dorm at Harvard University. He is a sought-after speaker. John McCain, one-time opponent, asked that Obama speak at his funeral, which he did in 2018.

Obama's **memoir**, *A Promised Land,* was published in late 2020. It was written by hand and covers Obama's life from 2004 to 2017. Michelle's memoir, *Becoming,* was published in 2018. Her husband supported her as she toured internationally to promote it.

Michelle Obama signs copies of her book *Becoming* in 2018.

Obama laughs with Joe Biden in the Oval Office.

The Obamas have also launched a film production company, Higher Ground Productions. They will work on projects around the issues of "race and class, democracy and civil rights, and much more." Sasha graduated from Sidwell Friends in June 2019. In August, she began college at the University of Michigan. As with Malia, the Obamas helped her move in to her dorm. In December, the Obamas bought a house on Martha's Vineyard, Massachusetts. The family spent part of every August there for seven of the eight years he was president.

Barack Obama is one of the most popular former presidents. His charisma, leadership, and empathy for those who are struggling continue to draw people to him. His desire to have Americans come together as a country continues to inspire many people.

Obama is left-handed. He was the eighth U.S. president in history who was known to be left-handed.

**When he was young, Barack went by "Barry"
to make it easier for other people to say.**
Why is a person's name important?
How might changing your name to help other people affect your identity?

In Hawaii, Barack was one of the few Black kids in school.
How was his experience different from his classmates'?

TIME LINE

1960

1961
Barack Hussein Obama is born on August 4 in Honolulu, Hawaii.

1980

1983
Graduates from Columbia University in New York City, New York.

1985
Works as a community organizer in Chicago, Illinois.

1990

1990
Becomes first African American to be elected as president of *Harvard Law Review*.

1991
Graduates from law school at Harvard University, becomes civil rights lawyer in Chicago, and later teaches law at the University of Chicago.

1992
Marries Michelle Robinson on October 18.

1996
Wins election to the Illinois Senate.

**Obama lives by the Golden Rule: Do unto others
as you would have them do unto you.**
Why might this rule be important as a leader?
In what ways could this rule be less important?

2000

2004
Delivers main speech at the Democratic National Convention, is elected U.S. senator for Illinois in November.

2005
Receives Grammy Award for Best Spoken Word Album for *Dreams from My Father*

2007
In February, Obama announces he will run for president of the United States.

2008
Receives Grammy Award for Best Spoken Word Album for *The Audacity of Hope: Thoughts on Reclaiming the American Dream* in February. In November, he is elected 44th president of the United States, the first African American to do so.

2009
Wins Nobel Peace Prize.

2010-PRESENT

2012
Wins second term as U.S. president in November.

2017
Leaves White House to become private citizen.

2019
Launches Higher Ground Productions with Michelle.

2020
Publishes his memoir *A Promised Land*.

anthropologist (an-thruh-POL-uh-jist)
An anthropologist is someone who studies people from different cultures. They want to know what they eat, how they dress, and what they believe.

charisma (kuh-RIZ-muh)
Charisma is a personal quality that gives someone influence over large numbers of people. Some people in leadership positions have charisma.

conservative (kuhn-SUR-vuh-tiv)
A conservative is a group or person in favor of keeping things the same. Conservatives often favor existing conditions.

democracy (deh-MOK-ruh-see)
Democracy is rule by the people. In America, we elect our officials by voting.

Great Depression (GRAYT dih-PRESH-uhn)
The Great Depression was an economic crisis in the U.S. and other countries. It began when the stock market crashed in 1929 and continued through the 1930s.

legislature (LEJ-iss-lay-cher)
A legislature is a body of elected people in a state or a country. They can make, change, or repeal laws. In America, we have state and national legislatures.

liberal (LIB-uh-ruhl)
A liberal is a group or person in favor of individual liberties. Liberals often favor change and progress.

lobby (LAHB-bee)
To lobby is to try to influence someone. In politics, lobbyists try to convince lawmakers to vote certain ways.

magna cum laude (MAHG-nuh KOOM LAUW-duh)
Magna cum laude means "with great distinction." When students graduate, they receive this honor if they have above-average grades.

memoir (MEM-wahr)
A memoir is an autobiography. Obama's memoir is called *A Promised Land.*

racism (RAY-sih-zum)
Racism is a negative feeling or opinion about people because of their race. Obama has dealt with racism all of his life.

recession (rih-SESH-uhn)
A recession happens when the economy slows down. Recessions are usually limited in scope and duration.

scholarship (SKAHL-ur-ship)
A scholarship is money given to students to continue studying. People get scholarships because they need money or because they got good grades.

swift kites (SWIFT KITES)
Swift kites are made of fabric and long, thin line. Players try to cut the line of their opponents' kites with their own line.

BOOKS

Freiberger, Paul. *All About Barack Obama.* Indianapolis, IN: Blue River Press, 2020.

Gilpin, Caroline Crosson. *Barack Obama.* Washington, DC: National Geographic, 2014.

Leslie, Tonya. *The Story of Barack Obama.* Emeryville, California: Rockridge Press, 2020.

Nichols, Catherine. *Barack Obama: Our 44th President.* Mankato, MN: The Child's World, 2021.

Obama, Barack. *Of Thee I Sing: A Letter to My Daughters.*
London, UK: Doubleday Children's, 2010.

Souza, Pete. *Dream Big Dreams: Photographs from Barack Obama's Inspiring and Historic Presidency.* New York, NY: Little, Brown and Company, 2017.

WEB SITES

Visit our website for links about Barack Obama:

childsworld.com/links

Note to Parents, Teachers, and Librarians: We routinely verify our Web links to make sure they are safe, active sites—so encourage your readers to check them out!

INDEX